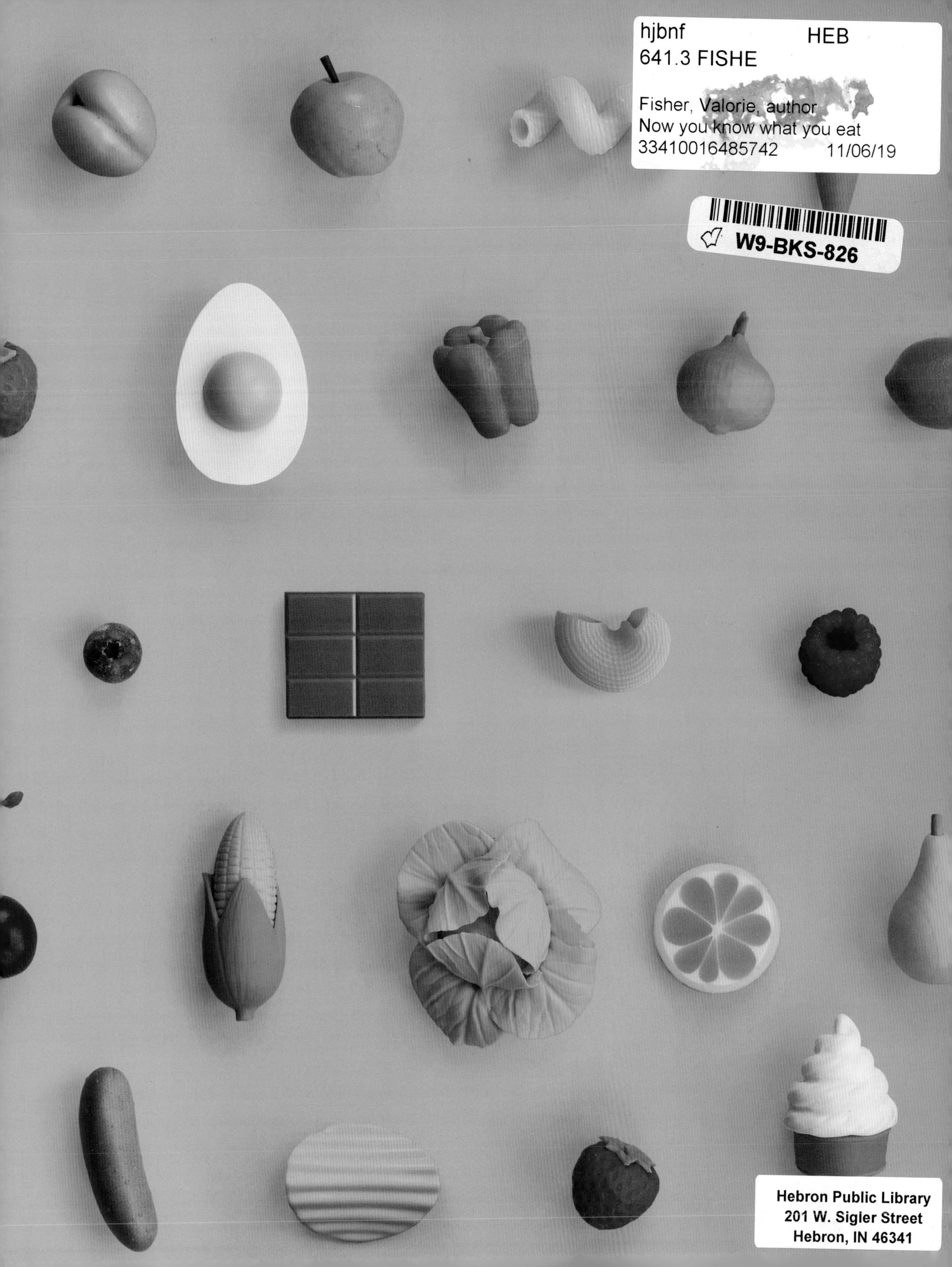

for Aidan & Olive

AUTHOR'S NOTE

For the purposes of creating this book, I chose simple and accessible explanations over depth and complexity so that it would be engaging and informative to the youngest of readers. My hope is that by revealing some of the science behind everyday foods, I will spark a child's curiosity and inspire them to keep asking, "What am I eating?"

Copyright © 2019 by Valorie Fisher

Book design by Valorie Fisher and Kirk Benshoff

Library of Congress Cataloging-in-Publication Data available
ISBN 978-1-338-21546-5
10 9 8 7 6 5 4 3 2 1
19 20 21 22 23
Printed in Malaysia 108
First edition, October 2019

Special thanks to Dr. Peter Wong, PhD, Director of Food Initiative and Special Assistant to the president at the Museum of Science in Boston, MA, for his guidance and expert verification of the information included in this book.

now you know

WHAT YOU EAT

valorie fisher

ORCHARD BOOKS · NEW YORK · AN IMPRINT OF SCHOLASTIC INC.

What's inside this book

How to read this book

$A + B = C$ A combination of A and B equals C.

$A - B = C$ A without B equals C.

$A \big\} B$ A comes from or can be found in B.

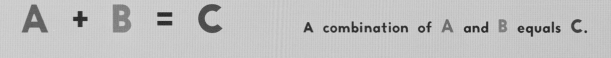   Solid line with an arrow shows direction of an object.

   At the bottom of some pages, you will find a circle with an image inside. This image means that a process or ingredient mentioned on this page has also been mentioned on the page with that image in the circle. Go to that circle's page to check it out!

Vanilla Ice Cream

vanilla ice cream =

cream
+
milk
+
sugar
+
eggs
+
vanilla extract

flour
+
sugar
+
eggs
+
butter

= cone

vanilla ice cream

chicken

wheat

cow

sugarcane

vanilla orchid

Milk

cow

calf

udder

teat

Female cows make milk after they have given birth to their first calf. Milk is stored in the udder and squeezed from the teats.

Cows are milked twice a day.

morning

In one week, a cow makes about 45 gallons of milk—enough to fill a bathtub.

afternoon

yogurt

butter

sour cream

cream

ice cream

cheese

milk

Brown Swiss   Holstein Guernsey

Ayrshire   Jersey

Some cows make more milk than others. These are called dairy cows.

Different parts of the world use the milk of other animals.

goat
Europe

sheep
Europe

llama
South America

camel
Africa
Middle East

water buffalo
India
Italy

reindeer
Scandinavia

2

Oatmeal Raisin Cookie

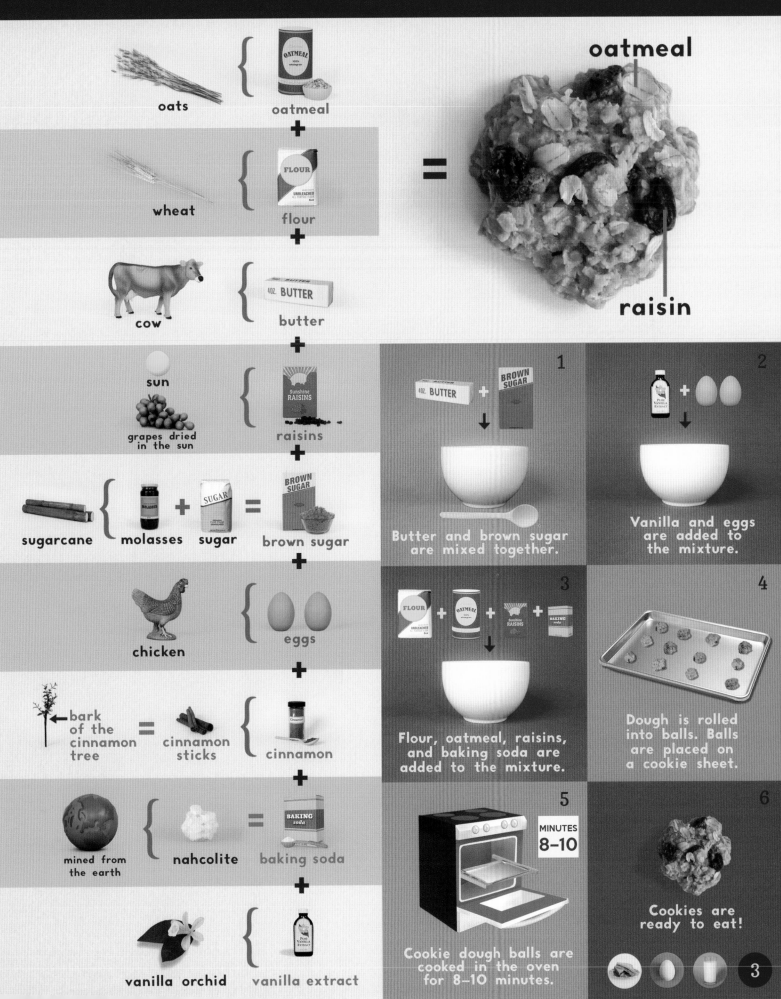

oats → oatmeal

+

wheat → flour

+

cow → butter

+

sun, grapes dried in the sun → raisins

+

sugarcane → molasses + sugar = brown sugar

+

chicken → eggs

+

bark of the cinnamon tree = cinnamon sticks → cinnamon

+

mined from the earth → nahcolite → baking soda

+

vanilla orchid → vanilla extract

oatmeal + flour + butter + raisins + brown sugar + eggs + cinnamon + baking soda + vanilla extract = **oatmeal raisin** cookie

1 Butter and brown sugar are mixed together.

2 Vanilla and eggs are added to the mixture.

3 Flour, oatmeal, raisins, and baking soda are added to the mixture.

4 Dough is rolled into balls. Balls are placed on a cookie sheet.

5 MINUTES 8–10 — Cookie dough balls are cooked in the oven for 8–10 minutes.

6 Cookies are ready to eat!

3

Peanut Butter & Jelly

peanut butter

grape jelly

whole wheat bread

grapevine = { grapes

+

fruit { pectin

Pectin is used to thicken jelly.

+

sugarcane { sugar

whole wheat flour =

Whole wheat flour uses the bran, the germ, and the endosperm of the wheat kernel. White flour only uses the endosperm.

wheat

kernel — endosperm
— bran
— germ

+

salt

evaporated from the sea — mined from the earth

+

water

+

yeast

Yeast is a fungus, a group of organisms that includes mold, mildew, and mushrooms. The yeast creates little pockets of carbon dioxide in the dough: This is called fermentation. The pockets make the dough rise.

Peanut Butter & Jelly

peanut shell

peanut

=

CREAMY PEANUT BUTTER

A peanut is not a nut, it is a legume. A legume is a plant with seeds that grow in pods. The peanut is the seed of the plant; each peanut pod, or shell, usually holds two peanuts.

flower

DAYS 2-3

sun

oven

peanuts

peanut

shoots

soil

CREAMY PEANUT BUTTER

Peanut seeds grow into green leafy plants with flowers. These flowers grow shoots that extend into the soil and form peanut pods underground.

When the peanuts are ready to be harvested, the plant is dug up with the peanuts and dried in the sun.

Peanuts are shelled, roasted, and have their skins removed.

Peanuts are ground into peanut butter.

Maple Syrup

maple syrup

PURE Maple Syrup

leaf

maple tree

seed

Maple leaves change color in the fall.

Maple Syrup

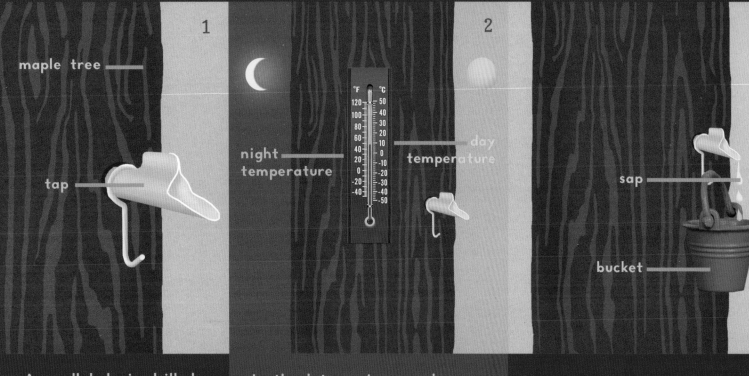

1

maple tree ——

tap ——

A small hole is drilled into the maple tree, and a tap, which acts as a spout, is inserted.

2

night temperature ——

—— day temperature

In the late spring, maple sap flows when nights are below 32°F and days are above 40°F.

3

—— sap

bucket ——

The sap is clear, watery, and sweet. Sap drips through the tap and into a bucket.

40 gallons of sap

4

40 gallons of sap = **1** gallon of syrup

5

6

=

Sap collected in buckets is boiled for many hours. The water in the sap slowly evaporates.

As the water evaporates, the color changes. It takes 40 gallons of sap to make 1 gallon of syrup.

The finished sap is golden brown.

Apple

leaf —

— stem

— seed

In spring, the apple tree sprouts blossoms. Honeybees fly from flower to flower pollinating the blossoms.

— bee

— blossom

In summer, the apples begin to grow.

young apple —

In fall, the apples are ripe and ready to be picked.

There are thousands of varieties of apples that grow all over the world.

mcintosh	golden delicious
granny smith	empire
honeycrisp	rome
jonagold	winesap
ginger gold	braeburn
paula red	russet
fuji	red delicious

40 apples

1 gallon of cider

Corn

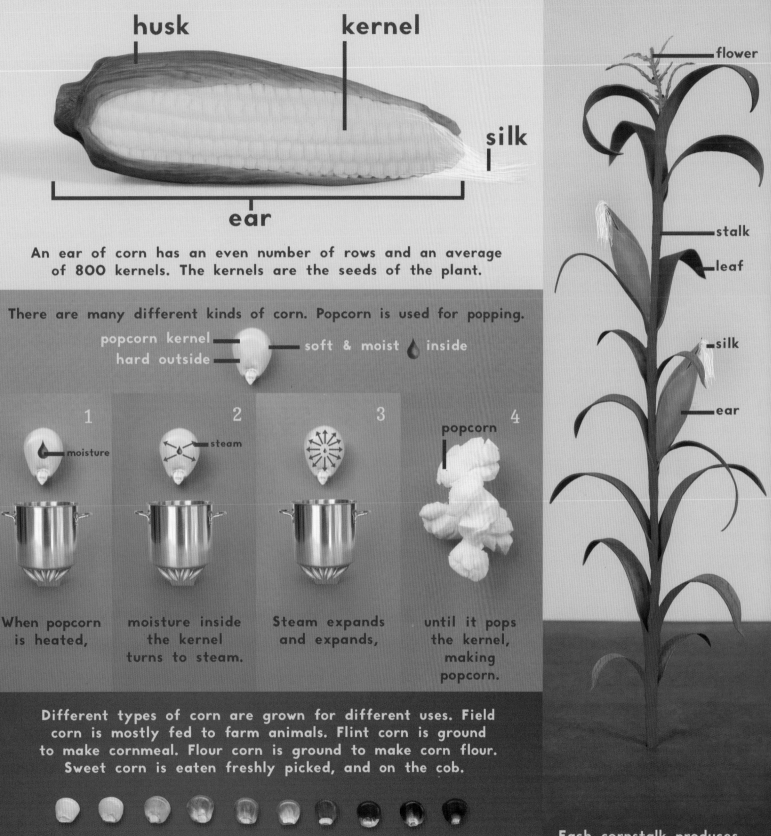

husk

kernel

silk

ear

An ear of corn has an even number of rows and an average of 800 kernels. The kernels are the seeds of the plant.

flower

stalk

leaf

silk

ear

There are many different kinds of corn. Popcorn is used for popping.

popcorn kernel
hard outside

soft & moist inside

1 moisture

2 steam

3

popcorn 4

When popcorn is heated,

moisture inside the kernel turns to steam.

Steam expands and expands,

until it pops the kernel, making popcorn.

Different types of corn are grown for different uses. Field corn is mostly fed to farm animals. Flint corn is ground to make cornmeal. Flour corn is ground to make corn flour. Sweet corn is eaten freshly picked, and on the cob.

Popcorn kernel colors vary, but they always pop white.

Each cornstalk produces one or two ears of corn.

Macaroni & Cheese

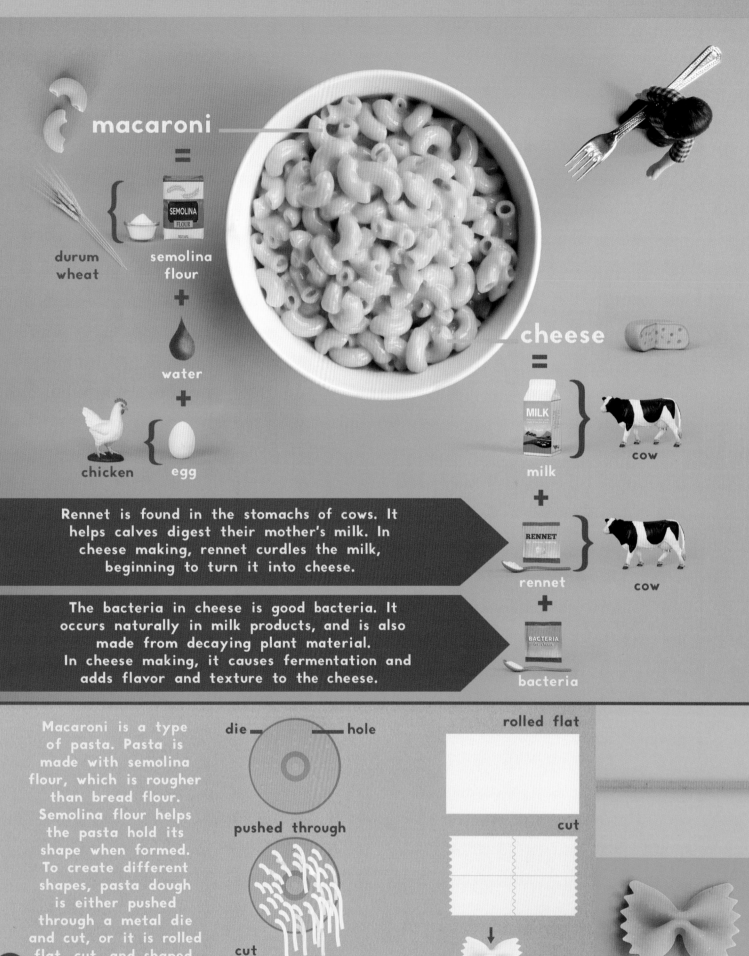

macaroni =

durum wheat { semolina flour

+

water

+

chicken { egg

cheese =

milk } cow

+

Rennet is found in the stomachs of cows. It helps calves digest their mother's milk. In cheese making, rennet curdles the milk, beginning to turn it into cheese.

rennet } cow

+

The bacteria in cheese is good bacteria. It occurs naturally in milk products, and is also made from decaying plant material. In cheese making, it causes fermentation and adds flavor and texture to the cheese.

bacteria

Macaroni is a type of pasta. Pasta is made with semolina flour, which is rougher than bread flour. Semolina flour helps the pasta hold its shape when formed. To create different shapes, pasta dough is either pushed through a metal die and cut, or it is rolled flat, cut, and shaped.

die — hole

pushed through

cut

rolled flat

cut

shaped

Macaroni & Cheese

1

To make cheese, milk is heated.

2

Bacteria is added, causing the milk to ferment and thicken.

3

Rennet is added, causing the milk to curdle. Curdled milk is lumpy and separates into **curds** and **whey**.

4

curds

whey

Whey, the watery liquid remaining after the milk curdles, is strained from the curds.

5

curds

curds

moisture

mold

Curds are pressed into molds, becoming more solid as they lose moisture.

6

cheese

DAY 1 to **YEAR 1**

Some cheeses are eaten fresh, but most cheeses are aged from a month to a year to develop flavor.

Cheese is often made with cow's milk, but it can also be made with milk of other animals.

cow

goat

sheep

water buffalo

camel

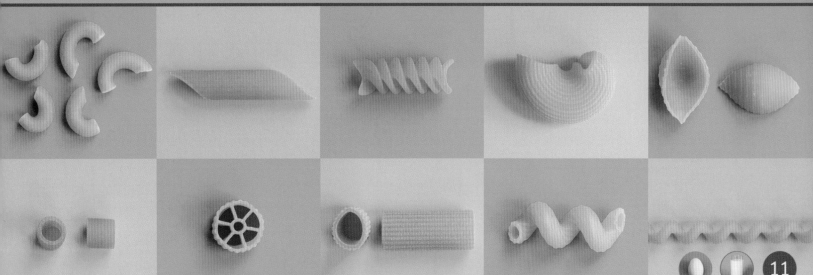

Chocolate

milk chocolate

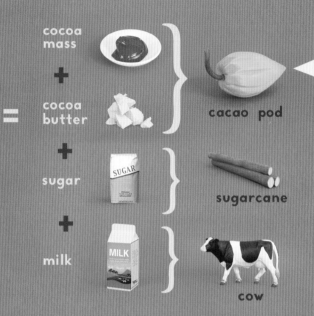

cocoa mass

+

cocoa butter

=

} cacao pod

+

sugar

} sugarcane

+

milk

} cow

dark chocolate

= − milk

white chocolate

= − cocoa mass

Chocolate

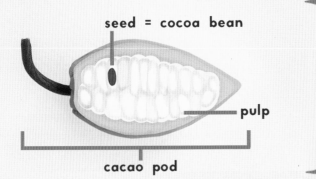

seed = cocoa bean

pulp

cacao pod

Inside the pod, a white, spongy pulp surrounds the seeds called cocoa beans.

Cacao pods grow on the trunk and branches of the cacao tree.

cacao pod

cacao tree

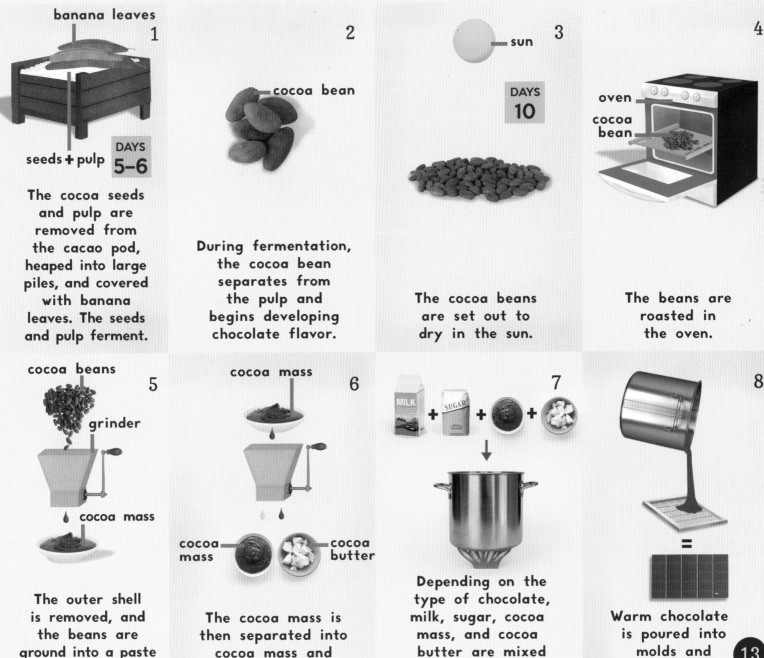

1

banana leaves

seeds + pulp

DAYS 5-6

The cocoa seeds and pulp are removed from the cacao pod, heaped into large piles, and covered with banana leaves. The seeds and pulp ferment.

2

cocoa bean

During fermentation, the cocoa bean separates from the pulp and begins developing chocolate flavor.

3

sun

DAYS 10

The cocoa beans are set out to dry in the sun.

4

oven

cocoa bean

The beans are roasted in the oven.

5

cocoa beans

grinder

cocoa mass

The outer shell is removed, and the beans are ground into a paste called cocoa mass.

6

cocoa mass

cocoa mass

cocoa butter

The cocoa mass is then separated into cocoa mass and cocoa butter.

7

MILK + SUGAR + ● + ▨

Depending on the type of chocolate, milk, sugar, cocoa mass, and cocoa butter are mixed and heated.

8

=

Warm chocolate is poured into molds and cooled.

Dill Pickle

dill pickle _____

=

seeds _____

cucumber **+** white vinegar **+** garlic **+** salt **+** dill **+** water

cucumber vine | corn | garlic bulb | earth | dill plant | earth

earth

sea

1
Liquids and salt are boiled over heat.

2
The cucumber, garlic, and dill are put into a jar.

3
The hot liquid is poured into the jar and it is sealed.

4
MINUTES
10
The jar is placed into boiling water for 10 minutes.

5
WEEK
1
The jar is removed from the hot water and set aside for at least one week.

6
Pickles are ready to eat!

Lemonade

lemon tree

Lemon trees grow in warm climates and produce fruit all year round.

sugarcane

lemonade = lemon + water + sugar

SUGAR

There are many kinds of citrus fruits.

lime   tangerine   kumquat   lemon   orange   grapefruit

1 A glass of water is combined with the juice from two lemons.

2 Two tablespoons of sugar are added to the mixture.

3 The liquid is stirred, and the lemonade is ready to drink!

4

Yogurt

yogurt = milk + bacteria

milk

bacteria

camel

cow or water buffalo

sheep

goat

1

Milk is heated.

2

Bacteria is added to the milk, causing it to ferment and curdle. This makes the milk thicken and develop a tangy taste.

or

3

The yogurt gets poured into containers where it cools, thickens, and sets.

Yogurt is eaten plain or sweetened, and often topped with fruit.

honey	maple syrup	strawberry	peach	blueberry	banana	raspberry
honeybee	maple tree	strawberry plant	peach tree	blueberry plant	banana plant	raspberry plant

Vegetable Soup

vegetable soup
=

flower
leaf
stem
fruit — seed
soil
root

A vegetable is any part of a plant we eat that does not have seeds, like leaves, stems, or roots. A fruit is any part of a plant we eat that has seeds. There are many foods that we think are vegetables but are actually fruits!

+ + + + +

seed
fruit
tomato

seed
=
fruit
corn

stem
celery

seed
fruit
kidney bean

leaf
parsley

seed
fruit
green bean

+ + + + +

root
carrot

flower
cauliflower

stem
onion

water

pepper

salt
SALT

earth

seed
fruit
pepper vine

earth
earth
sea

Egg

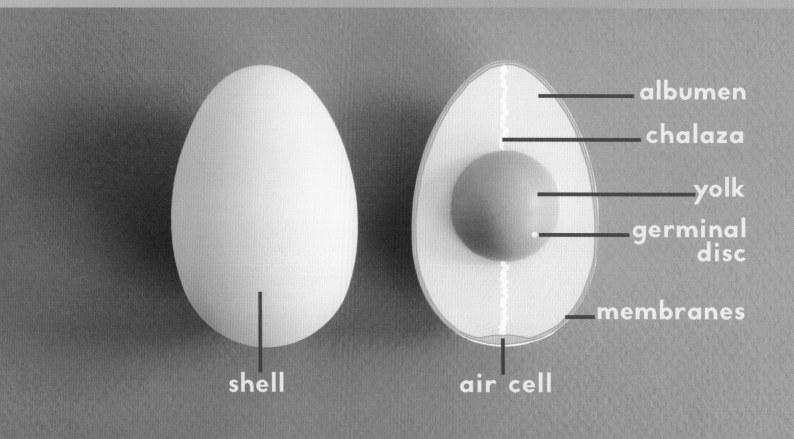

albumen

chalaza

yolk

germinal disc

membranes

shell

air cell

egg

Eggs are strong. If your weight is evenly balanced, you can stand on an upright egg and it won't crack!

We eat several different kinds of eggs.

quail   chicken   duck   goose

Egg

earlobe

comb

tail

beak

wattle

hen

A male chicken is a rooster, and a female chicken is a hen. Only hens lay eggs, usually one a day, but less in winter. In an average year, a hen lays **276** eggs.

Different breeds lay different color eggs. Eggshell colors vary, but inside, the eggs are the same.

Maran   Easter Egger   Leghorn   Ameraucana   Rhode Island Red   Olive Egger

All eggshells start off as white, but in some breeds the shell is dyed as it passes through the hen. Some eggshells are dyed inside and out, and others are only dyed on the outside.

Pizza

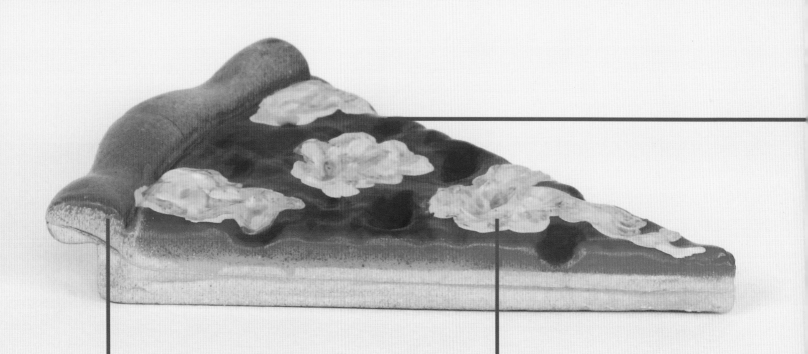

crust

=

flour + wheat

+

olive oil + olive

+

salt + sea earth

+

yeast

+

water

mozzarella cheese

=

milk + water buffalo **or** cow

+

salt + earth sea earth

+

rennet + cow

+

citric acid + citrus fruit

Citric acid is found in citrus fruit. The acid helps separate the milk into curds and adds texture.

Mozzarella is eaten fresh, not aged.

Pizza

tomato sauce

tomato sauce =

tomato + garlic + salt + pepper + olive oil + basil

tomato → tomato plant

garlic → garlic bulb

salt

pepper

olive oil → olive

basil → basil plant

TOMATO SAUCE

SALT

OLIVE OIL

salt

Salt is collected from evaporated seawater. Shallow pools of seawater dry up in the hot sun, leaving only salt.

Salt is dug from salt mines deep inside the earth.

sun

salt mine

Peppercorns grow on the pepper vine in hot climates. They are dried in the sun, becoming black and wrinkly.

Peppercorns are crushed and ground into pepper.

1

sun

DAYS 10

pepper vine

peppercorns

=

2

peppercorns + pepper grinder

=

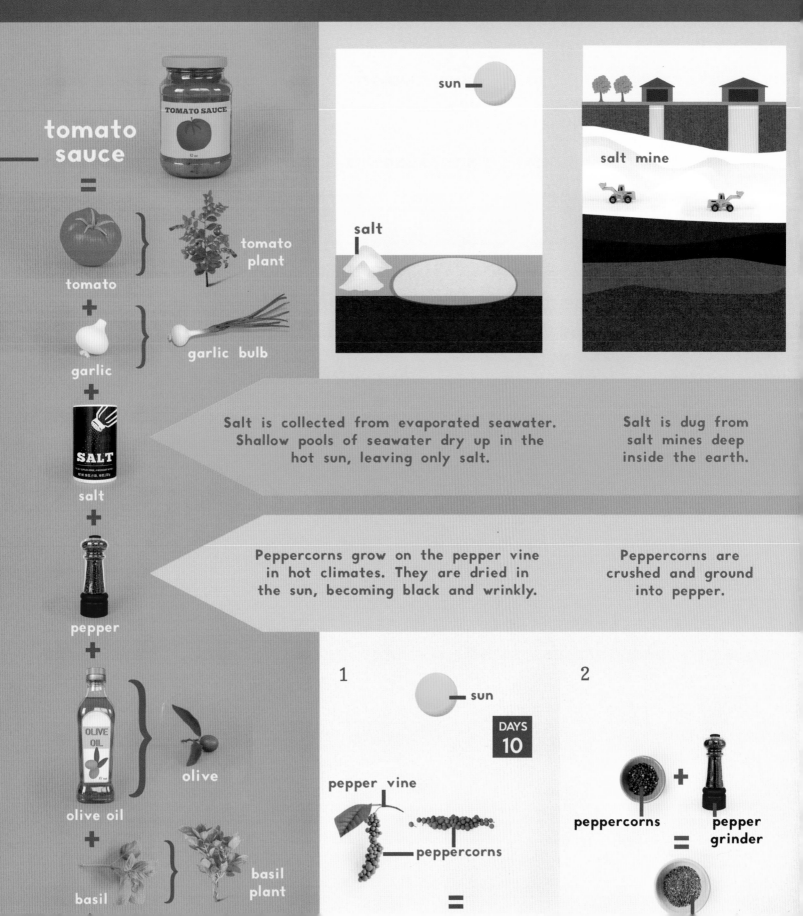

Honey

honeybee

abdomen —————————————— wing

mandible —
proboscis —

The proboscis is a straw-like tongue used for sucking nectar, a sugary substance found in flowers. The mandible, or jaw of the bee, helps it eat, chew, clean, cut, feed, and fight.

honeybee
The honeybee is striped, fuzzy, and small.

bumblebee
The bumblebee, while also fuzzy, has blocks of color and is larger than a honeybee.

yellow jacket
The yellow jacket is striped like the honeybee, but it's not a bee at all—it's a wasp!

Honey

honeybee —   hive

honeycomb

Honeybees have different jobs. One important job is to make the honeycomb. It is built from wax, made from the honey they eat, which is stored in their abdomens. The bees push the wax out of their abdomens in flakes. They chew the flakes until the wax is soft and easy to mold, and use it to create the cells of the honeycomb.

Some honeybees fly from flower to flower collecting nectar and bringing it back to the hive. The nectar is passed by mouth to a bee at the hive who chews it, helping it begin to evaporate. Then it is put into the cells of the honeycomb. The bees fan the cells with their wings, helping the moisture evaporate even more. Soon it thickens into honey. When a cell is full, a bee will cap the cell with wax to seal the honey in.

honeycomb

honey — cell

A cell is a 6-sided shape called a hexagon.

1
honeycomb
knife
caps
frame

Wax caps are removed from the honeycomb.

2
extractor

Honeycombs are placed into an extractor.

3
Inside the extractor, the honeycombs are spun to separate the honey from the comb.

4
Honey is filtered and put into jars.

flowers to make one jar of honey.

Potato Chip

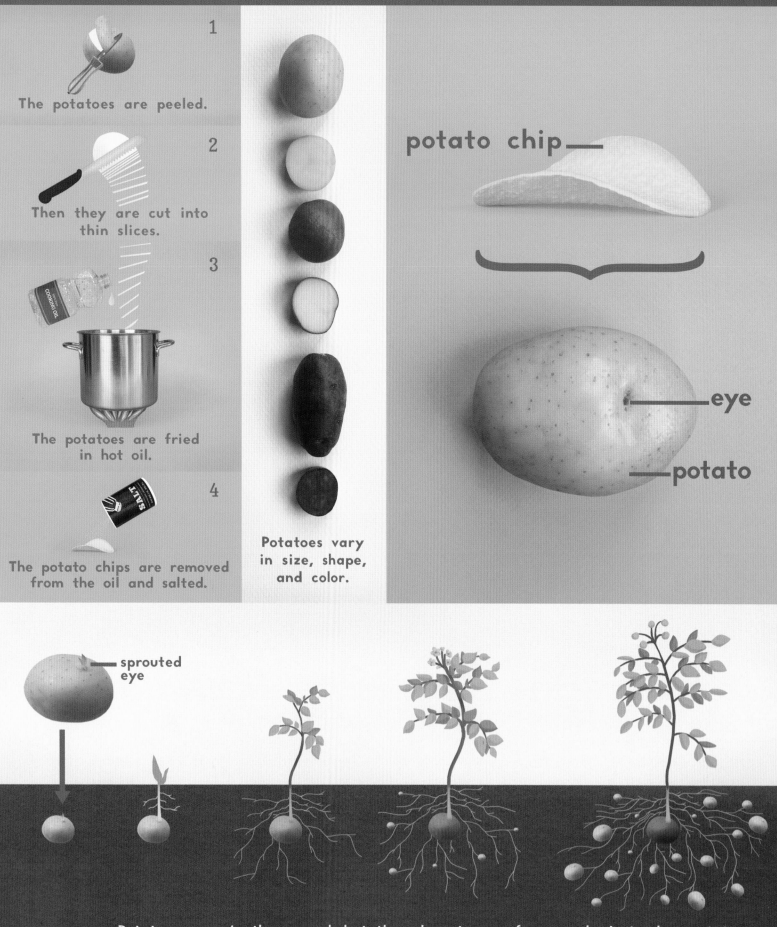

1 The potatoes are peeled.

2 Then they are cut into thin slices.

3 The potatoes are fried in hot oil.

4 The potato chips are removed from the oil and salted.

Potatoes vary in size, shape, and color.

potato chip

eye

potato

sprouted eye

Potatoes grow in the ground, but they do not grow from seeds. Instead, a potato with a sprouted eye is planted. The tiny sprout grows into a leafy plant above the ground. Underground, the plant grows roots. New potatoes grow on these roots.

What's on your plate

Eating a variety of foods from all five food groups at every meal is important to growing strong and staying healthy.

dairy
- yogurt
- ice cream
- milk
- cheese

fruit
- orange
- watermelon
- apple
- avocado
- pear
- grapes
- raisins
- tomato
- apricot
- berries
- banana

grain
- cereal
- rice
- pancake
- croissant
- bread
- oatmeal
- pasta
- bagel
- tortilla
- corn muffin
- waffle

vegetable
- potato
- cauliflower
- beet
- onion
- carrot
- sweet potato
- beans
- cabbage
- celery
- peas
- spinach
- broccoli
- kale
- garlic
- lettuce

protein
- beef
- nuts
- beans
- egg
- tofu
- fish
- peanut butter
- chicken

Vitamins & Minerals

The vitamins and minerals in foods are very important. They help your body grow strong and stay healthy. They help with a variety of functions and body parts depending on the vitamin or mineral.

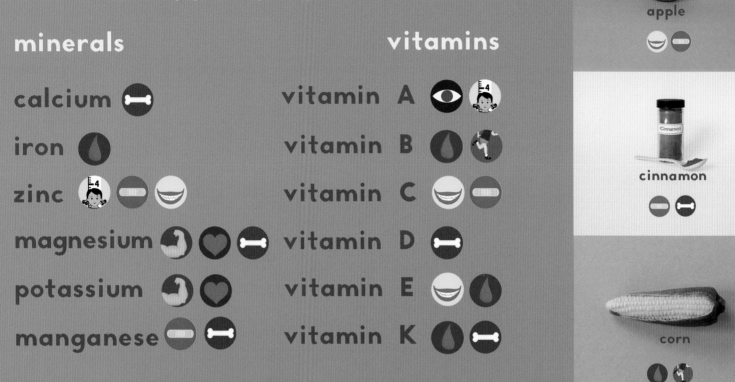

minerals

calcium

iron

zinc

magnesium

potassium

manganese

vitamins

vitamin A

vitamin B

vitamin C

vitamin D

vitamin E

vitamin K

HOW TO READ THIS PAGE

Use the symbols below to help understand how vitamins and minerals help your body grow strong and stay healthy.

eyes

muscle

heart

growing

blood

bones & teeth

healing wounds

stay healthy

energy

apple

cinnamon

corn

berries

ice cream

peach

Vitamins & Minerals

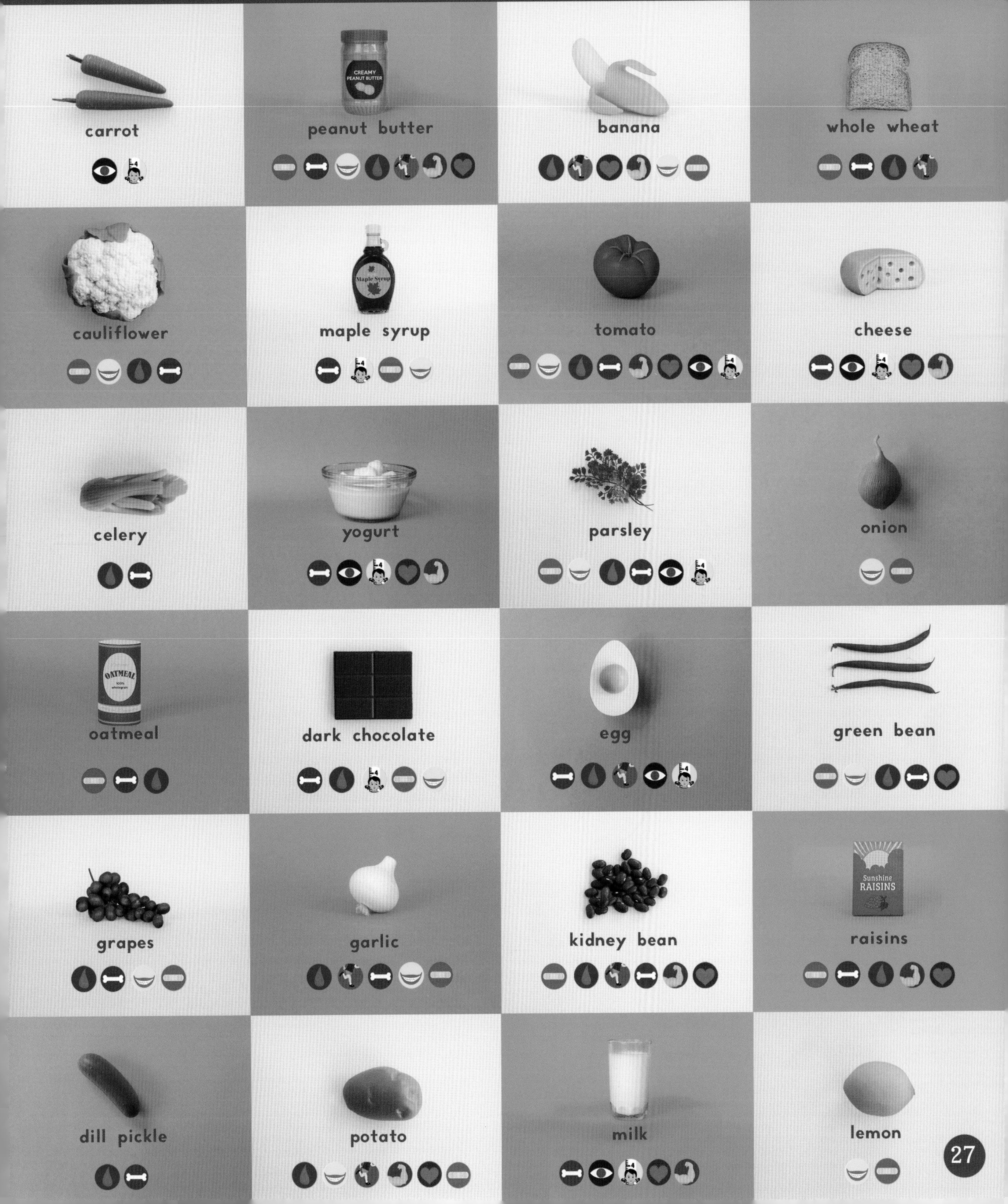

carrot
CREAMY PEANUT BUTTER
peanut butter
banana
whole wheat
cauliflower
Maple Syrup
maple syrup
tomato
cheese
celery
yogurt
parsley
onion
OATMEAL
oatmeal
dark chocolate
egg
green bean
grapes
garlic
kidney bean
Sunshine RAISINS
raisins
dill pickle
potato
milk
lemon

Words to Know

bacteria

Bacteria are tiny living things, so small you can't see them, that live all around and inside soil, water, plants, and animals.

decay

To decay is to rot. Decaying apples under the tree attract many wasps.

wasp
decaying apple

baking soda

Baking soda is a fine powder used in baking that reacts to heat and acids, creating carbon dioxide bubbles. The bubbles trapped in the dough cause it to rise, making fluffy and light cakes, breads, and cookies.

BAKING soda

digest

To digest is to break down food in the stomach so that it can be absorbed into the body.

carbon dioxide

Carbon dioxide is an odorless, tasteless gas. Baking soda creates carbon dioxide bubbles in baking. Carbon dioxide bubbles are also found in soda.

carbon dioxide bubbles

fermentation

Fermentation is a chemical change of a substance often by bacteria or yeast. Fermentation often produces heat and carbon dioxide bubbles.

chocolate

yogurt

curdle

To curdle is the thickening and separation of milk into lumps called curds and liquid called whey.

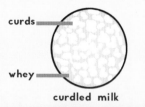

curds

whey

curdled milk

evaporation

Evaporation is the change of a liquid into a gas that leaves the surface. The hot sun evaporates the puddle of water.

1   2   3   4

puddle   puddle   puddle

extractor

An extractor is a machine used to separate honey from the honeycomb. The extractor spins the honeycomb very quickly, causing the honey to spin free of the honeycomb.

nectar

Nectar is a sweet liquid found in flowers. Nectar helps attract birds and insects to flowers, which helps with pollination.

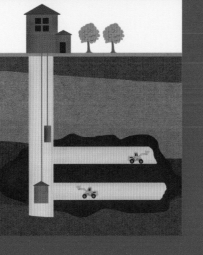

nectar

flower

mine

A mine is a deep hole or series of tunnels dug into the earth from which rocks and minerals are dug.

pectin

Pectin is a substance found in some fruits, often in the peel or rind. Pectin helps thicken jellies and jams as they cook.

apple peel

lime rind

mineral

Minerals are chemical substances, such as iron, zinc, and salt, found in foods that are important for good health. Minerals occur naturally in foods and in the earth.

iron   zinc   salt

pollination

Pollination is the movement of pollen, usually by insect, bird or wind, from one flower to another, which helps the plant produce seeds.

grains of pollen

honeybee

nahcolite

Nahcolite is a white mineral, which is ground into a fine powder and used as baking soda.

BAKING soda

nahcolite

vitamin

Vitamins are natural substances found in food, which are important for growth and good health. Eating foods high in vitamins helps you have lots of energy to play!